# One Dough Fifty Cookies

## Baking Favorite and Festive Cookies in a Snap

### Leslie Glover Pendleton

William Morrow and Company, Inc.
New York

*To Mark, William, and Lydia*
*My tireless tasters and loving supporters*

Copyright © 1998 by Leslie Glover Pendleton
Illustrations copyright © 1998 by Tom Glover

It is the policy of William Morrow and Company, Inc., and its imprints and affili-
ates, recognizing the importance of preserving what has been written, to print the
books we publish on acid-free paper, and we exert our best efforts to that end.

Library of Congress Cataloging-in-Publication Data

Pendleton, Leslie Glover.
    One dough fifty cookies : baking favorite and festive cookies in a snap / Leslie
Glover Pendleton.
        p.    cm.
    ISBN 0-688-15443-3
    1. Cookies.   2. Baking.   I. Title.
TX772.P38      1998
641.8'654—dc21                                                              98-17818
                                                                                CIP

PRINTED IN THE UNITED STATES OF AMERICA

FIRST EDITION

1 2 3 4 5 6 7 8 9 10

BOOK DESIGN BY LISA STOKES

www.williammorrow.com

# Acknowledgments

I have been blessed with family and friends who travel with me on a continually exciting journey in the world of creative food. I thank all of you who have patiently tasted endless dozens of cookies.

I am most grateful to my father, Tom Glover, whose creative gifts and character have inspired me throughout my life. His contribution to this book is lovingly appreciated. And to my mother, Diane, whose talent and love of cooking were patiently passed on to me and who generously helped with the final testing of these recipes.

Many thanks to my friends at *Gourmet* magazine. I have learned more from you than I had ever imagined possible. Especially Romulo Yanes, who graciously agreed to team up with me again to shoot the cover, and Zanne Stewart, Kemp Minifie, and Diane Keitt, who continue to support me with encouragement and constructive criticism. Finally, I thank Alice Martell, whose energy and enthusiasm helped me through to the very last batch.

# Contents

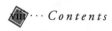

# Introduction

One simple dough. One perfectly balanced, delectable butter cookie dough is all you need to produce dozens of distinctly different but equally delicious freshly baked cookies. If you were to strip away the different flavors and textures from many of the classic cookies around the world, you would be left with a basic butter cookie. The first to disappear from a holiday sampler, and devoured by the pound from those blue Danish cookie tins, the butter cookie is a universal favorite. Now here is a way to start with that simple dough, and with it create new classics by the dozens that are suitable for everything from silver trays to lunch boxes.

Start with one large master batch of butter cookie dough, and divide it in half. Each recipe that follows calls for one half of the Master Dough. Stir lime zest and almonds into one half, form into sticks, and coat with sugared almonds for a sophisticated petit four. Into the other half stir chocolate chips, brown sugar, and egg whites for Good, Old-fashioned Chocolate-Chip Cookies, and you've thrilled your dinner guests and your children at the same time. Only want to make one cookie? Then chill or freeze the remaining dough for another time.

What better time for simplified baking than during the hectic holidays? In a quick, organized fashion you can produce beautiful platters of assorted cookies without having to start from scratch each time. Have them on hand (for months in the freezer) for last-minute holiday or hostess gifts. Maybe the most amazing part of this trick is that the cookies taste and look completely different from each other. No one will suspect you've taken a shortcut.

This is also a fun way to cook with children. Batches of dough can be made ahead of time and each child can choose the flavors and shapes to make their own unique cookies.

Once you start, you'll want to make more and more all of the time!

# Helpful Hints to Get Started

**1** Using a heavy-duty electric mixer or a food processor is the best way to make the dough. Of course, you can mix by hand, but it will be a workout.

**2** Measuring precisely is very important in baking. Tired of hearing this? Well, tough. No shortcuts here! To measure flour and sugar, use granulated, dry-ingredient measuring cups (the kind that fit inside of each other). Do not use a liquid measuring cup. Spoon the ingredient into the cup and level off with a straight edge. Do not sift, pack, or shake the cup. In the same manner, level off the dry ingredients in measuring spoons. Brown sugar should be measured in dry measuring cups and packed firmly until level with the rim.

**3** Measure 5 cups of flour into a separate bowl and remove ¼ cup (to yield 4¾ cups), when measuring for the Master Dough. You should not measure directly into the mixing bowl, because it is very easy (in fact, likely) to lose count of the cups.

**4** Do not throw away the egg whites that are left over from the Master Dough until you've checked the subrecipe. If the recipe calls for egg whites (many of them do), it will either call for 3 egg whites or a cup measurement in order to make use of those extras.

**5** Do not worry about washing the mixing bowl when making more than one variety at a time. But if one dough is messier than the other—such as the softer drop cookie doughs—mix the less messy first.

**6** Make batches of the Master Dough in advance, if desired, and evenly divide them. Keep the dough well wrapped in layers of plastic and foil. It can be chilled for up to one week, or frozen for up to three months. Let the dough come to room temperature before mixing or forming.

**7** If at any time the dough becomes too soft to work with, especially in warm, humid weather, chill and wrap the dough for 15 to 30 minutes, or until firm enough to handle.

**8** Do not grease the baking sheets unless otherwise specified. Just wipe them clean and let them cool between batches.

**9** Use nonstick cookie sheets, if you wish, but be aware that dark surfaced sheets can cause cookies to brown and crisp faster. If at any time the cookies cool too long and stick on the baking sheet, return the sheet to the oven for 30 seconds to 1 minute and the cookies will come free.

**10** Store the cookies in airtight containers: at room temperature, 3 days; in the refrigerator, 2 weeks; in the freezer, as long as 8 weeks. Layer fragile or glazed cookies between sheets of wax paper before storing.

**11** Use either a grater or a zester when zesting lemon, lime, orange, or grapefruit. A zester is a hand-held tool with small holes lined up along a metal edge that is dragged across the zest. Make sure to get only the very thin, colored, outer part of the rind, for when the white pith is included, it produces a bitter taste. One lemon yields, at the most, about 1 teaspoon zest. A lemon should still look yellow after it is zested.

**12** There is a general misconception that spices and dried herbs never go bad, and therefore, can be kept forever. However, they actually lose their flavor and unique character rather quickly. Therefore, buy them in small quantities, store them in airtight containers, and replace them when they lose their potency.

**13** Nuts and seeds are also ingredients that need special handling. The high fat content in nuts makes them turn rancid easily. Seeds, such as poppy and sesame seeds, also go "off" quickly. Store all nuts and seeds in double heavy-duty sealable plastic bags in the freezer. Be sure to taste them before using them.

**14** *For the recipes in this book*:

*Brown sugar* Use either light or dark brown.

*Molasses* Use either unsulphured or dark.

*Flour* Use either bleached or unbleached all-purpose.

*Oats* Use either old-fashioned rolled or quick-cooking.

*Cocoa* All of the recipes were tested with nonalkali cocoa, such as Hershey's. If Dutch-processed cocoa with alkali is used, it could produce a different result.

*Instant espresso powder* This is a wonderful ingredient, which provides a deep, rich, coffee flavor and dissolves easily. If you cannot find it in your supermarket, ask the store to carry it. Freeze-dried instant coffee crystals can be substituted, but be sure to crush the crystals to a powder in order to get an accurate measurement.

**15** Look for hard-to-find baking supplies such as pearl sugar, chocolate-covered coffee beans, and colored sugars in Mail-Order Sources (page 95).

# The Master Dough

*This recipe provides enough dough to make two variations of cookies.* If you only want to make 1 batch of cookies, freeze the unused half of the Master Dough for another time.

*4 sticks (1 pound) unsalted butter, softened slightly*
*1⅓ cups sugar*
*1 teaspoon salt (use ¾ teaspoon if using salted butter)*
*3 large egg yolks*
*2 teaspoons pure vanilla*
*4¾ cups flour (see hint 3, page xi)*

When using a heavy-duty electric mixer fitted with the paddle attachment:

In a large bowl, cream together the butter, sugar, and salt. Add the egg yolks and vanilla and beat until smooth. Add the flour gradually, beating on low speed until incorporated.

When using a food processor fitted with a steel blade and with a bowl capacity of 11 cups or more:

In the food processor, blend the flour,

> Note: Do not allow the butter to soften too much, as the resulting dough will also be soft and harder to work with. Margarine is not recommended.
>
> Use common sense when mixing in additional ingredients. Coarse ingredients will be chopped by the blade (in a food processor), and should be stirred in by hand in a separate bowl.

sugar, butter (cut into small pieces), and salt until the mixture is crumbly. Add the yolks and vanilla, and blend the mixture, scraping the bowl occasionally, until it forms a dough.

# SPRITZ AND HAND-FORMED COOKIES

# Classic Spritz Cookies

MAKES ABOUT 7 DOZEN

*This cookie is the mother of all butter cookies. The idea for this* entire book sprang from the universal adoration of these perfectly formed, tender, buttery treats. Here, the basic dough is forced through a "spritzer," or a cookie press, which forms distinct shapes. I use my late great-great-aunt's, and one bought at a garage sale. My aunt filed down the legs of her "spritzer" during the war so her precious butter- and sugar-laden cookies would be thinner, and she could get twice the amount! Both of my cookie presses extrude the dough as the top is screwed down. Specialty kitchen supply stores carry European-made types that extrude the dough by squeezing a lever. Try to avoid electric or battery-operated models. Once you get the hang of using a spritzer, it is easy to turn out hundreds of different shapes.

*½ recipe Master Dough (page 1)*
*¼ cup egg whites, lightly beaten with 2 teaspoons water*
*Decorations: colored sugars or sprinkles, chopped nuts,*
*sliced glacéed cherries and other glacéed fruits*

Preheat the oven to 350°F.

Fit the canister of a cookie press with the desired cutting disc. Then fill it with some of the dough. Press out the cookies 1 inch apart on cool, clean, ungreased baking sheets.

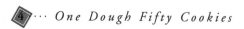

Brush the cookies lightly with the egg white and decorate as desired.

Bake the cookies for 12 to 14 minutes, or until the edges are pale golden. Let the cookies cool on the sheets for 1 minute. Transfer the cookies to wire racks to cool completely. Do not let the cookies cool too long on the sheets or the egg whites and sugar will cause them to stick.

There are three important tips to keep in mind when "spritzing":

1. Use the dough right after mixing. (It is tricky getting the dough to the right temperature and consistency after chilling.)

2. "Spritz" onto a clean, cool baking sheet. Wash the sheets between batches; you want the dough to stick to the sheets.

3. Work confidently and quickly, pressing the dough onto the sheet, and jerking the press quickly to the side and lifting, to break off the dough.

# Mocha Butter Balls

□□□□ □□□□ □□□□ □□□□ □□□□ □□□□ □□□□

*This is an adaptation of a recipe I have been making for Christ-*mas since 1973. The original one was featured in the annual *Woman's Day* magazine holiday cookie collection. These balls are rolled in confectioners' sugar while still warm, giving them a thin, buttery frosting.

*½ recipe Master Dough (page 1)*
*¼ cup unsweetened cocoa powder*
*2 teaspoons instant espresso powder*
*1 cup finely chopped walnuts or pecans*
*Approximately 2 cups confectioners' sugar*

Preheat the oven to 350°F.

In a large bowl, beat together the dough, cocoa powder, espresso powder, and nuts with an electric mixer on medium speed until thoroughly combined.

Roll the dough into 1-inch balls and arrange them ¾ inch apart on ungreased baking sheets.

Bake the cookies until they are just firm and beginning to brown, 16 to 20 minutes. Let the cookies cool for 5 minutes on the sheets.

> Note: Before the balls are stored or frozen, they can be lightly coated again with confectioners' sugar to prevent them from sticking to each other.

In a large bowl, whisk the confectioners' sugar (or sift if sugar is very lumpy). While the cookies are still warm, working with about 6 at a time, coat them with the sugar by swirling them around in the bowl. Transfer to sheets of wax paper to cool completely.

# Zesty Lime and Almond Sticks

MAKES ABOUT 9 DOZEN

$A$ light coating of egg white, sugar, and almonds forms a crisp exterior around the delicate, flaky, tangy interior. These are very popular with adults as well as children. It is fun to watch people's faces while trying to identify the familiar tasting lime flavor.

1 cup whole natural almonds
½ recipe Master Dough (page 1)
1½ teaspoons freshly grated lime zest
1 tablespoon fresh lime juice
¾ cup confectioners' sugar
3 large egg whites, lightly beaten with ¼ teaspoon salt

Preheat the oven to 350°F. Grease the baking sheets.

In a food processor, process the almonds until finely ground.

In a large bowl, beat together the dough, lime zest, juice, and ½ cup of the ground almonds with an electric mixer on medium speed until thoroughly combined. Chill the dough, if necessary, until firm enough to roll.

In a bowl, blend together the remaining ground almonds and confectioners' sugar.

> Note: Lime zest is even trickier to grate than lemon because it's thinner. Make sure to get only the green part of the rind, not the bitter white pith. Your limes should still have a light green coating on them when you're done.

Roll pieces of dough into ½-inch-thick ropes. Cut the ropes into 2-inch lengths. Coat each one with egg white and roll in the almond sugar. Arrange the cookies ¾ inch apart on the prepared baking sheets.

Bake the cookies for 16 to 18 minutes, or until they are very pale golden. Carefully transfer the cookies to wire racks to cool.

# Orange Marmalade Walnut Pillows

## MAKES ABOUT 9 DOZEN

*The pieces of sweet, chewy orange peel found in marmalade are a* perfect match for these aromatic, spicy cookies. It is also a timesaving alternative to making candied orange peel from scratch.

*One 18-ounce jar orange maramlade*
*½ recipe Master Dough (page 1)*
*2 cups ground walnuts*
*1½ teaspoons baking powder*
*1 cup confectioners' sugar*
*1 teaspoon ground cinnamon*
*¼ teaspoon ground cloves*

Preheat the oven to 350°F.

In a small saucepan, melt the marmalade and press it through a fine sieve with the back of a spoon. The solids should measure about ¾ cup. Save the leftover jelly for another use (see Note).

In a large bowl, beat together the dough, marmalade solids, walnuts and baking powder

> Note: The leftover strained preserves can be saved, chilled in the jar, and used as a jelly for toast or a glaze brushed over ham or poultry when cooking.

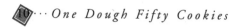

with an electric mixer on medium speed until thoroughly combined. Chill the dough, if necessary, until it is firm enough to roll.

Roll level teaspoonfuls of the dough into balls and arrange them ¾ inch apart on ungreased baking sheets.

Bake the cookies for 14 to 16 minutes, or until they just begin to turn golden. Let the cookies cool for 2 minutes.

In a large bowl, whisk (or sift if sugar is lumpy) together the confectioners' sugar, cinnamon, and cloves. Working with about 6 warm cookies at a time, coat them with spiced sugar by swirling them around in the bowl. Transfer the cookies to sheets of wax paper to cool completely.

# Sambuca Coffees

## MAKES ABOUT 6 DOZEN

*T*he heavenly combination of aniseed, espresso, and Sambuca make these sophisticated cookies a real treat with an after-dinner cup of coffee. You also receive the added delight of the chocolate-covered coffee bean inside this delicious morsel.

*½ recipe Master Dough (page 1)*
*2 tablespoons aniseeds, ground in a spice or coffee grinder*
*2 tablespoons instant espresso powder*
*2 tablespoons Sambuca liqueur (optional)*
*½ cup confectioners' sugar, plus additional for dusting the cookies*
*Approximately 72 chocolate-covered espresso beans (about 8 ounces)*

Preheat the oven to 350°F.

In a large bowl, beat together the dough, ground aniseed, espresso powder, Sambuca, and confectioners' sugar with an electric mixer on medium speed until thoroughly combined.

Push 1 chocolate-covered espresso bean into rounded teaspoonfuls of the dough and roll them into balls. Arrange them ¾ inch

Note: Chocolate-covered espresso beans or coffee-flavored chocolate coffee beans (which can also be used) are available at specialty food stores, coffee shops, and some supermarkets. See also page 95 for Mail-Order Sources.

apart on ungreased baking sheets.

Bake the cookies for 15 to 18 minutes, or until they just begin to turn golden. Transfer the cookies to wire racks to cool and dust the cookies with confectioners' sugar by shaking it through a sieve.

# Malted Milk Buttons

□□□□ □□□□ □□□□ □□□□ □□□□ □□□□ □□□□

These cookies are reminiscent of malted milk balls, my favorite candy to have at the movies. These funny-looking little cookies are sure to please.

*½ recipe Master Dough (page 1)*
*2 cups Ovaltine malt or chocolate malt–flavored powder*
*½ teaspoon salt*
*6 ounces milk chocolate*

Preheat the oven to 350°F.

In a large bowl, beat together the dough, malt powder, and salt with an electric mixer on medium speed until thoroughly combined.

Roll ½ teaspoonfuls of the dough into balls and arrange them ¾ inch apart on ungreased baking sheets.

Bake the cookies for 12 to 14 minutes, or until just firm. Transfer the cookies to wire racks to cool.

In a bowl set over a saucepan of simmering water, melt the chocolate, stirring often. (Chocolate can also be melted in a microwave, heating 30 seconds at a time, stirring often.)

Dip the tops of the cookies into the chocolate, lifting straight up to form a chocolate "kiss." Let the chocolate set. (Cookies can be chilled to harden the chocolate faster.)

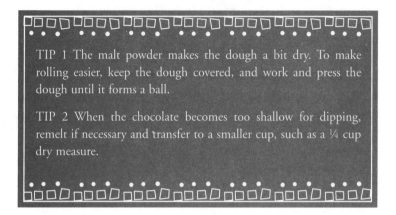

TIP 1 The malt powder makes the dough a bit dry. To make rolling easier, keep the dough covered, and work and press the dough until it forms a ball.

TIP 2 When the chocolate becomes too shallow for dipping, remelt if necessary and transfer to a smaller cup, such as a ¼ cup dry measure.

# Jelly Bowls

These old-fashioned "thumbprint" cookies, also called "birds in the nest" and "jam tarts," can be filled with any jam that you like. For a sweet surprise, drop a chocolate chip in the center of each cookie before adding the jam.

*½ recipe Master Dough (page 1)*
*¾ cup strawberry, raspberry, or apricot jam*

Preheat the oven to 350°F.

Roll the dough into 1-inch balls, and arrange them 1 inch apart on ungreased baking sheets.

Using your finger, make an indentation in the center of each ball. Fill each with about ¼ teaspoon jam.

Bake the cookies for 14 to 16 minutes, or until the edges are pale golden. Let the cookies cool on the sheets for 2 minutes. Transfer the cookies to wire racks to cool completely.

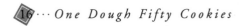

# Shattered Chocolate Balls

MAKES ABOUT 6 DOZEN

*R̶olling these deep, dark chocolate cookies in confectioners' sugar* before baking produces an attractive cracked surface when they come out of the oven.

*½ recipe Master Dough (page 1)*
*½ cup unsweetened cocoa powder*
*2 teaspoons baking powder*
*½ cup granulated sugar*
*3 large egg whites*
*Approximately 1 cup confectioners' sugar*

> Note: For the best contrast between the sugar and chocolate, do not shake off any excess sugar after rolling, even though it may seem like too much.

In a large bowl, beat together all the ingredients except the confectioners' sugar with an electric mixer on medium speed until thoroughly combined. Chill the dough for 2 hours, or until firm.

Preheat the oven to 350°F.

Sift the confectioners' sugar into a medium-size mixing bowl. Roll the dough into 1-inch balls, dropping them into the sugar. Shake the bowl to coat the balls generously and arrange them ¾ inch apart on ungreased baking sheets.

Bake the cookies for 14 to 17 minutes, or until the tops are cracked and the cookies are cooked through. Transfer the cookies to wire racks to cool.

# Almond Crescents

I*n high school, I was an American Field Service exchange student* living with a family in Austria, in a small town just south of Vienna. The recipe for these cookies (known in Austria as *vanillekipferl*) was one of many I collected during my visit. The first time I made these delicacies back home was at Christmas, when a favorite food-loving uncle was visiting. One late night, my mother and I could not figure out what bizarre sound was coming from the kitchen, until we realized my uncle had discovered the box of freshly baked almond crescents and was wholeheartedly devouring them!

*1⅔ cups almonds*
*½ cup granulated sugar*
*¼ teaspoon salt*
*½ recipe Master Dough (page 1)*
*1½ teaspoons almond extract*
*Approximately 3 cups confectioners' sugar*

Preheat the oven to 350°F.

In a food processor, process the almonds, granulated sugar, and salt until finely ground.

In a large bowl, beat together the almond mixture, dough, and extract with an electric mixer on medium speed until thoroughly combined.

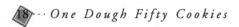

Roll the dough into 3-inch-long ropes and form into crescents, arranging them ¾ inch apart on ungreased baking sheets.

Note: The crescents need to cool slightly on baking sheets. They are very fragile right after baking, but they firm up when cooled. After freezing or chilling, the cookies can be given a fresh dusting of confectioners' sugar.

Bake the cookies for 12 to 14 minutes, or until pale golden, and let them cool for 5 minutes on the sheets.

Sift some confectioners' sugar onto a large tray. Transfer the slightly warm crescents to the tray and sift more sugar on top. Shake the tray to coat them lightly with sugar. When they are cool, transfer the crescents to storage containers, shaking off any excess sugar.

# Orange Date Oatmeal Crisps

## MAKES ABOUT 7 DOZEN

*The idea for forming cookies this particular way comes from eastern Europe and Scandinavia, where terra-cotta molds are used to press decorative designs into cookies. If you have one of these cookie molds, use it in the same manner as the glass and dip it in sugar. Either way, this is a fun and easy way to make uniform cookies with a tasty and attractive sugar coating. It is also a job that kids will love to help with.*

*½ recipe Master Dough (page 1)*
*1 cup chopped dried, pitted dates*
*¾ cup old-fashioned or quick rolled oats*
*1½ teaspoons freshly grated orange zest*
*Approximately ½ cup sugar*

> Note: If the cookies cool and stick to the sheets, return them to the oven for 1 minute to soften.

Preheat the oven to 350°F.

In a large bowl, beat together the dough, dates, oats, and zest with an electric mixer on medium speed until thoroughly combined.

Roll the dough into 1-inch balls and roll them in sugar. Arrange the balls 2 inches apart on ungreased baking sheets. Flatten them to form 2-inch rounds with the bottom of a buttered glass dipped in sugar.

Bake the cookies for 12 to 14 minutes, or until pale golden. Immediately transfer the cookies to wire racks to cool.

# Russian Tea Cakes

## MAKES ABOUT 8 DOZEN

*Also known as Mexican tea cakes or Mexican wedding cakes, these* short, buttery balls are another universal favorite. For as long as I can remember, my mother's friends have had competitions over whose buttery nut cookie was better. To this day, they are all convinced that theirs is the superior cookie. I am confident that there will never be a clear-cut winner. You just can't go wrong with these delectable classics.

½ recipe Master Dough (page 1)
½ cup confectioners' sugar plus approximately 2 cups
   confectioners' sugar
1 cup chopped pecans or walnuts
1 teaspoon baking powder
½ cup cornstarch

Preheat the oven to 350°F.

In a large bowl, beat together the dough, ½ cup confectioners' sugar, nuts, baking powder, and cornstarch with an electric mixer on medium speed until thoroughly combined.

Roll the dough into 1-inch balls and arrange them ¾ inch apart on ungreased baking sheets.

Note: Before the balls are stored or frozen, they can be coated again lightly in confectioners' sugar to keep them from sticking to each other.

*continued*

Bake the cookies for 14 to 16 minutes, or until just firm and beginning to brown. Let the cookies cool for 5 minutes on the sheets.

Put the additional confectioners' sugar in a large bowl and while the cookies are still warm, swirl 6 at a time in the bowl until they are coated with sugar. Transfer them to sheets of wax paper to cool completely.

# Lemon Poppyseed Pillows

MAKES ABOUT 7 DOZEN

These pretty glazed, speckled cookies are a lovely addition to a summer picnic or a delicious accompaniment to a cool glass of lemonade or iced tea.

½ recipe Master Dough (page 1)
½ cup poppy seeds
½ cup honey
¾ teaspoon freshly grated lemon zest
½ teaspoon almond extract
½ teaspoon baking soda
1⅓ cups confectioners' sugar
¼ cup fresh lemon juice

In a large bowl, beat together the dough, poppy seeds, honey, zest, extract, and baking soda with an electric mixer on medium speed until thoroughly combined. Chill the dough for 1 hour, or until it is firm enough to roll.

Preheat the oven to 350°F.

Roll level teaspoonfuls of the dough into balls and arrange them ¾ inch apart on ungreased baking sheets.

Note: It is very important to grate lemon zest correctly in order to obtain the desired tangy lemon flavor without any bitterness. (See hint 11, page xiii.)

*continued*

*Spritz and Hand-Formed Cookies* ···

Bake the cookies for 14 to 16 minutes, or until they begin to turn golden. Transfer the cookies to wire racks to cool slightly.

In a small bowl, whisk together the confectioners' sugar and lemon juice until smooth. While still warm, dip the top of each cookie into the glaze, letting the excess drip off. Transfer the cookies to wire racks set over wax paper and let them stand at room temperature until the glaze is hardened.

# Berry Gem Tartlets

## MAKES 6 DOZEN

▢▢▢▢ ▢▢▢▢ ▢▢▢▢ ▢▢▢▢ ▢▢▢▢ ▢▢▢▢ ▢▢▢▢

T*he plain butter cookie dough has also classically posed as the per-*fect crust for fresh fruit tarts. Miniature tart shells can be frozen and defrosted for a last-minute but impressive dessert. You can serve the tartlets with a dollop of whipped cream and a mint sprig, or just plain to be eaten out of hand.

*½ recipe Master Dough (page 1)*
*¾ cup currant jelly*
*Fresh berries, such as hulled strawberries,*
  *blueberries, raspberries, or blackberries*
  *(1 pint of berries fills slightly more than 1 dozen*
  *shells)*

Note: There is enough dough to fill two 8-inch tart pans, but they must bake 20 to 30 minutes, or until golden. Also, line the bottoms with rounds of parchment to ensure easy removal.

Preheat the oven to 375°F.
Press rounded teaspoonfuls of the dough onto the bottom and up the sides of ⅛-cup miniature muffin tins.

Bake shells for 15 minutes, or until golden brown. Let them cool for 10 minutes. Turn shells out onto wire racks and let cool completely.

In a small saucepan, simmer jelly, stirring, for 1 minute. Brush hot jelly inside shells and top with some berries. (Stand single, whole strawberries trimmed side down.) Brush hot jelly over berries and let it set. The tartlets can be assembled 8 hours in advance, kept uncovered, and chilled.

# Granola Bars

Granola *cereal is a convenient ingredient that adds nutrients,* fruits, nuts, and an extra touch of sweetness, not to mention a satisfying crunch, to cookies. Try different granolas paired with a different mix of grains and fruit. You may even want to supplement your cookies with additional raisins, dates, or nuts.

*½ recipe Master Dough (page 1)*
*3 cups regular or low-fat granola cereal with fruit*
*½ cup firmly packed brown sugar*

Preheat the oven to 350°F. Line an 8-inch-square baking pan or dish with plastic wrap.

In a large bowl, beat together all the ingredients with an electric mixer on medium speed until thoroughly combined.

Press the dough firmly into the baking pan, and chill, if necessary, until it is firm enough to cut.

Turn the dough out onto a clean work surface and discard the plastic. Using a long serrated knife, cut the dough gently with a sawing motion into ¼-inch-thick slices. Cut each slice into four 2-inch bars and arrange them ¾ inch apart on ungreased baking sheets.

Bake the cookies for 14 to 17 minutes, or until pale golden. Transfer the cookies to wire racks to cool.

# ICEBOX COOKIES

# Chocolate-Dipped Coconut Sticks

MAKES ABOUT 12 DOZEN

*T**hese delicate, crunchy treats are a guaranteed crowd pleaser. The* best way to form perfect sticks is to make the final cut directly on the cookie sheets.

2½ *cups sweetened flaked coconut*
½ *recipe Master Dough (page 1)*
2 *cups chocolate chips or chopped semisweet chocolate*

Preheat the oven to 350°F.

Spread the coconut in a large shallow baking pan and toast it in the oven, stirring occasionally, about 10 minutes, or until golden. Let it cool completely.

In a large bowl, beat together the coconut and dough with an electric mixer on medium speed until thoroughly combined. Divide the dough in half and between 2 sheets of wax paper, pat it into 11 × 2½-inch rectangles. Wrap the dough in the wax paper and chill until firm, about 30 minutes.

Working with 1 rectangle of dough at a time, cut it crosswise into ¼-inch-thick slices and arrange them 1 inch apart on ungreased baking sheets. Using a sharp knife, cut each slice in half lengthwise to form sticks, separating them slightly.

Bake the cookies for 13 to 18 minutes, or until pale golden. Let them cool slightly on the sheets. Transfer the cookies to wire racks to cool completely.

In a bowl set over a saucepan of simmering water, melt the chocolate, stirring occasionally. (The chocolate can also be melted in a microwave, heating 30 seconds at a time, stirring often.) Transfer the chocolate to a cup. Dip 1 end of each stick in the chocolate, drag the underside against the cup's rim to remove any excess, and transfer to wax paper to harden.

# Cappuccino Wafers

## MAKES ABOUT 9 DOZEN

These thin, delicate wafers pack an intense coffee flavor, guaranteed to please any java enthusiast. The raw dough logs can be kept double-wrapped in the freezer, providing a quick and easy way to have freshly baked cookies any time.

¼ cup instant espresso powder (see hint 14, page xiii)
1 tablespoon warm water
½ recipe Master Dough (page 1)
½ teaspoon baking soda
¼ cup sugar
¾ teaspoon ground cinnamon

In a small bowl, stir the espresso powder and water together until dissolved.

In a large bowl, beat together the dough, espresso, and the baking soda with an electric mixer on medium speed until thoroughly combined.

Divide the dough in half and on 2 sheets of wax paper, form the dough into two 10-inch-long logs, about 1½ inches in diameter. (If the dough is too soft to work with, chill it for 30 minutes.) Wrap the logs in wax paper or plastic and chill 1 hour, or until firm.

Preheat the oven to 350°F.

Stir the sugar and cinnamon together. Using a sharp knife, slice the logs ⅛ inch thick, and press 1 side of each slice gently into the cinnamon sugar. Arrange the slices ¾ inch apart, sugar side up, on ungreased baking sheets.

Bake the cookies for 10 to 12 minutes, or until crisp. Immediately transfer the cookies to wire racks to cool. (If the cookies cool and stick to the sheets, return to the oven for 1 minute.)

# Graham Cracker Honey Washboards

## MAKES ABOUT 6 DOZEN

*T*hese simple and tasty cookies are definitely the ideal comfort food for anyone. A couple of these washboards, served with a tall glass of milk, have been known to cure a woe or two and brighten up many a rainy day.

*½ recipe Master Dough (page 1)*
*1½ cups graham cracker crumbs*
*¼ cup honey*
*½ teaspoon freshly grated nutmeg*
*1 teaspoon ground cinnamon*

In a large bowl, beat together all the ingredients with an electric mixer on medium speed until thoroughly combined.

Divide the dough in half and on 2 sheets of wax paper, form the dough into two 8 × 4-inch bricks and wrap in wax paper or plastic wrap. Chill for 1 hour, or until firm.

Preheat the oven to 350°F.

Using a long, sharp knife, cut the bricks in half lengthwise, forming 4 logs 8 inches long and 2 inches wide. Cut the logs crosswise into ¼-inch-thick slices, and arrange them ¾ inch apart on ungreased baking sheets. Press the back of a fork into each slice to form ridges, dipping the fork in flour if it sticks.

Bake the cookies for 10 to 12 minutes, or until firm. Transfer the cookies to wire racks to cool.

# Tangy Lemon Wedges

## MAKES ABOUT 12 DOZEN

$T$*o achieve the truly eye-opening delicious lemon tang in these* delicate wafers, it is very important to grate the lemon zest correctly! If any white pith from the rind is included, it will produce a bitter, unpleasant flavor.

*½ recipe Master Dough (page 1)*
*1 tablespoon freshly grated lemon zest (from about 3 lemons)*
*3 tablespoons fresh lemon juice*
*⅓ cup yellow decorating sugar or sanding sugar*
   *(see Mail-Order Sources, page 95)*

In a large bowl, beat together the dough, zest, and juice with an electric mixer on medium speed until thoroughly combined.

On a sheet of wax paper or plastic wrap, form the dough into one 10-inch-long log about 2½ inches in diameter. Wrap the dough in wax paper or plastic wrap and freeze for 3 hours, or until firm. (If the dough is too soft to form a perfect log, remove and roll it into shape after freezing for 30 minutes.)

> Note: If yellow decorating sugar is not available, you can substitute ⅓ cup granulated sugar, mixed with ½ teaspoon turmeric. Ground turmeric is a vivid yellow spice which will brightly color the cookies as well as add a subtle complementary flavor to the lemon.

Preheat the oven to 350°F. Grease the baking sheets.

Using a sharp knife, cut the log crosswise into ⅛-inch-thick rounds, arranging slices ¾ inch apart on the prepared baking sheets. (Return any uncut dough to the freezer.) Sprinkle the rounds with about ¼ teaspoon of the yellow sugar and spread evenly with the tip of a finger.

Bake the cookies for 12 to 14 minutes, or until the edges just begin to turn golden. While the cookies are still hot on the sheets, cut rounds in half with a pizza or pastry wheel or a sharp knife. Transfer the cookies to wire racks to cool.

# Bitter Chocolate Almond Cookies

## MAKES ABOUT 8 DOZEN

*The large amount of cocoa and almonds in this recipe yields a dry crumbly cookie packed with plenty of chocolate flavor. If you cannot get coarse sugar, use regular granulated sugar or none at all.*

½ recipe Master Dough (page 1)
½ cup unsweetened cocoa powder
1 cup sliced almonds
1 teaspoon almond extract
⅓ cup granulated sugar
½ cup coarse decorating sugar

In a large bowl, beat together all the ingredients except the coarse sugar with an electric mixer on medium speed until thoroughly combined.

Divide the dough in half and on 2 sheets of wax paper, form the dough into two 8- to 9-inch-long logs. Sprinkle with the coarse sugar and roll the logs to coat evenly. Flatten the logs slightly to form oval slices. Wrap the logs in wax paper or plastic wrap and chill for 1 hour, or until firm.

Note: Coarse and pearl sugars are used primarily by commercial bakeries. Both are attractive and add a nice, extra sweet crunch, but regular granulated sugar can be substituted. (See Mail-Order Sources, page 95.)

Preheat the oven to 350°F.

Using a sharp knife, slice the logs ¼ inch thick. Arrange the slices ½ inch apart on ungreased baking sheets.

Bake the cookies for 15 to 18 minutes, or until crisp. Transfer the cookies to wire racks to cool.

# Chocolate Marzipan Pinwheels

## MAKES ABOUT 7 DOZEN

$M$*arzipan is slightly sweeter than almond paste and will give the* chocolate part a crisper texture, but either can be used here.

*½ recipe Master Dough (page 1)*
*7 ounces (about ⅔ cup) marzipan or almond paste, broken into small pieces*
*¼ cup unsweetened cocoa powder*
*1 tablespoon egg white*
*½ teaspoon almond extract*

Measure ½ cup of firmly packed Master Dough and transfer it to a bowl. Add the marzipan, cocoa, egg white, and almond extract and beat with an electric mixer on medium speed until smooth. This will take a few minutes.

Roll the remaining Master Dough out between 2 sheets of wax paper into a rectangle measuring about 10 × 15 inches. Roll out the chocolate dough between 2 sheets of wax paper to the same size. Remove the top sheet of paper and invert the chocolate dough onto the plain dough, pressing them together lightly. Remove the top sheet of paper and

> Note: Another way to form these doughs is to roll the plain dough into 2 rectangles, sandwich the chocolate layer in between, and cut the dough into sticks using a pizza wheel. Or try rolling the logs in chopped almonds.

starting with a long side, roll the dough up tightly, jelly-roll fashion, using the paper to help. Continue to roll and compress the log in the paper until it measures about 19 inches long. Chill for 2 hours, or until firm.

Preheat the oven to 350°F.

Using a sharp knife, slice the log into ¼-inch-thick slices. Arrange the slices ½ inch apart on ungreased baking sheets.

Bake the cookies for 15 to 20 minutes, or until pale golden. Transfer the cookies to wire racks to cool.

# Peanut Butter and Jelly Sandwiches

MAKES ABOUT 7 DOZEN

*These* cookies look like, taste like, and are just as addictive as PB&J sandwiches. Do not substitute fruit spread or sugar-free jelly, because the sugar is necessary for the jelly to set properly. But feel free to try melted chocolate.

*½ recipe Master Dough (page 1)*
*1 cup chunky-style peanut butter*
*1 cup whole wheat flour*
*¾ cup firmly packed brown sugar*
*2 tablespoons lightly beaten egg whites*
*1 teaspoon baking soda*
*1 cup grape or other jelly*

In a large bowl, beat together all the ingredients except the jelly with an electric mixer on medium speed until thoroughly combined.

Divide the dough in half and on 2 sheets of wax paper, form the dough into two 12-inch-long squared-off logs. Wrap in wax paper and chill for 4 hours or overnight.

> Note: It's hard to get two identical logs; the slices from one log won't match up well with slices from the other.

Preheat the oven to 350°F.

Using a sharp knife, cut the logs into slices slightly thicker than ⅛ inch. Arrange the slices ½ inch apart on ungreased baking sheets.

Bake for 14 to 18 minutes, or until pale golden. Transfer the cookies to wire racks to cool.

In a saucepan, melt the jelly over medium heat. Boil it for 5 minutes, stirring constantly, and transfer it to a bowl. Let the jelly cool about 5 minutes, or until it begins to set but is still hot.

Arrange half the cookies bottom side up. Top with ½ teaspoon jelly and sandwich with another cookie, pressing just until the jelly is visible at the edges. Let the cookies set for about 2 hours.

# Rugelach Spirals

MAKES ABOUT 6 DOZEN

$T$*raditional rugelach is a delectable fruit- and-nut-filled pastry* found on nearly every Jewish holiday table. These spirals are now hands down the favorite on my holiday sampler. The usual method of filling and rolling each cookie into a croissant shape is time-consuming and results in perhaps a larger-than-desired size. However, this adaptation makes forming the cookies quicker, produces small neat spirals, and uses less butter! The traditional dried currants or raisins can be used in place of the cranberries, as well as dried apricots or a mixture of dried fruits and other nuts.

*1 cup chopped pecans*
*1 cup chopped walnuts*
*1 cup chopped dried cranberries*
*2 teaspoons ground cinnamon*
*½ cup firmly packed brown sugar*
*2 tablespoons egg white (1 large)*
*½ recipe Master Dough (page 1)*

In a small bowl, stir together the nuts, cranberries, cinnamon, brown sugar, and egg white until thoroughly combined.

Divide the dough in half and form each half into a rough log shape. Working with one half at a time, roll the dough out between 2 sheets of wax paper into a rectangle measuring 8 × 17 inches. Remove the top sheet of paper and spread half of the nut mixture evenly on the surface, patting and pressing it lightly into the dough. Starting with a long side, roll the dough up tightly, jelly-roll fashion, using the paper to help. Wrap it in the wax paper and chill the logs for 1 hour, or until firm.

Preheat the oven to 350°F.

With a serrated knife, slice the logs ¼ to ½ inch thick. Arrange the slices ½ inch apart on ungreased baking sheets.

Bake the cookies for 19 to 22 minutes, or until pale golden. Transfer the cookies to wire racks to cool.

Note: Rolling up the dough can be tricky, but it gets easier with practice. Don't be afraid to really press the roll together and shove any loose filling in the ends. The nice thing about these cookies is even the messiest and loosest roll-up. Once they are sliced and baked, you get cookies that hold together and taste great.

# Benne Seed Honey Wafers

Sesame seeds, also known as benne seeds, are used in a traditional southern cookie. This variation produces a crisp wafer that has a delicate nutty taste. Be sure to use fresh sesame seeds because they can turn rancid quickly, and store them in an airtight container in the freezer in order to prolong freshness.

¾ cup sesame seeds
½ recipe Master Dough (page 1)
¼ cup honey
⅓ cup firmly packed brown sugar
¾ teaspoon baking soda

Preheat the oven to 350°F.

In a baking pan, toast the sesame seeds in the oven, stirring occasionally, for 8 to 10 minutes, or until pale golden. Let them cool slightly.

In a large bowl, beat together all the ingredients, including the cooled sesame seeds, with an electric mixer on medium speed until thoroughly combined.

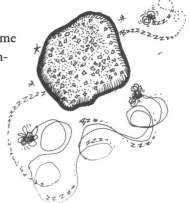

Divide the dough in half and on 2 sheets of wax paper, form the dough into two 12-inch-long logs. Wrap the logs in wax paper or plastic wrap and chill for 2 hours, or until firm.

Using a sharp knife, slice the logs ⅛ inch thick, and arrange the slices 1 inch apart on ungreased baking sheets.

Bake the cookies for 12 to 15 minutes, or until pale golden. Transfer the cookies to wire racks to cool.

# Spiced Peanut Currant Cookies

## MAKES ABOUT 7 DOZEN

The inspiration for the unusual combination of molasses, peanuts, currants, and allspice comes from Jamaican cuisine. These flavors complement one another beautifully, plus they dazzle the palate. The simple orange glaze is literally the frosting on the cake, but, of course, you may leave it off if desired.

½ recipe Master Dough (page 1)
¾ cup dried currants
¾ cup lightly salted peanuts
3 tablespoons molasses
1 teaspoon ground cinnamon
½ teaspoon ground allspice
¼ teaspoon freshly grated nutmeg
1 cup confectioners' sugar
2 tablespoons fresh orange or lemon juice

Beat together all the ingredients except the confectioners' sugar and juice in a large bowl with an electric mixer on medium speed until thoroughly combined.

Divide the dough in half and on 2 sheets of wax paper, form the dough into two 12-inch-long logs. Wrap the logs in wax paper and chill for at least 2 hours or overnight.

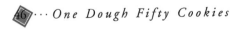

Preheat the oven to 350°F.

Using a sharp knife, cut the logs into ¼-inch-thick slices, and arrange them ½ inch apart on ungreased baking sheets.

Note: An easy way to decorate: Arrange the cookies on a sheet of wax paper, as close together as possible. Spoon the icing into a sealable plastic bag, expelling the air, and with scissors, snip off a tiny piece of the corner of the bag. Press the icing out the small hole, drizzling it back and forth over all of the cookies at once.

Bake the cookies for 13 to 17 minutes, or until pale golden. Immediately transfer the cookies to wire racks to cool.

In a small bowl, whisk together the confectioners' sugar and orange juice until smooth. Drizzle over the cookies and let the icing set (see Note).

# Cinnamon Chocolate Moons

In Mexican recipes, cinnamon and chocolate are classically paired in both sweet and savory dishes. The sharp spiciness of the cinnamon and the bittersweet smoothness of the chocolate make a sophisticated flavor combination. It is the perfect accompaniment to a cup of steaming espresso or cappuccino.

½ recipe Master Dough (page 1)
2½ teaspoons ground cinnamon
¾ cup sugar
8 ounces bittersweet chocolate

In a large bowl, beat together the dough, cinnamon, and sugar with an electric mixer on medium speed until thoroughly combined.

Divide the dough in half and on 2 sheets of wax paper, form the dough into two 12- to 13-inch-long logs. Wrap the logs in wax paper and chill for at least 4 hours or overnight.

Preheat the oven to 350°F. Grease the baking sheets.

Using a sharp knife, cut the logs into slices slightly more than ⅛ inch thick. Arrange the slices ½ inch apart on the prepared baking sheets.

Bake the cookies for 12 to 14 minutes, or until pale golden. Immediately transfer the cookies to wire racks to cool.

In a bowl over a saucepan of simmering water, melt the chocolate, stirring occasionally. (Chocolate can also be melted in a microwave, heating 30 seconds at a time, stirring often.) Transfer the chocolate to a cup. Dip half of each cookie in the chocolate, letting the excess drip off, and drag the underside against the cup's rim to remove any excess. Transfer the cookies to wax paper to harden.

Store the cookies in single layers separated by sheets of wax paper.

Note: For a clean, aromatic cinnamon flavor, buy high-quality cinnamon or grind new cinnamon sticks (not the ones that have been in the spice cabinet since you moved them from the old house) in a spice grinder.

Note: Experiment by dipping the cookies in more or less chocolate, creating different stages of the moon.

# ROLLED OR CUTOUT COOKIES

# Deep Chocolate Wafers

MAKES ABOUT 9 DOZEN

*These thin round wafers are as close to Nabisco's Original Chocolate Wafers as they can get! Coffee and coconut add an extra-rich depth to the chocolate flavor.*

*Rolling out the dough while soft makes it easier to get it thin; freezing the dough makes it easier to work with. If the sheets of dough get too soft at any time, return to the freezer for a few moments.*

*¾ cup sweetened flaked coconut*
*½ recipe Master Dough (page 1)*
*¾ cup unsweetened cocoa powder*
*¼ cup strong coffee (or ¼ cup water mixed with 1½ teaspoons instant espresso powder)*
*½ cup sugar*
*½ teaspoon baking soda*

Preheat the oven to 350°F.

In a shallow baking pan, toast the coconut in the oven for 10 minutes or until brown, stirring occasionally, and let cool. Crush and crumble the coconut until finely ground. (Or put the coconut in a plastic bag and crush with a rolling pin.)

In a large bowl, beat together all the ingredients, including the coconut, with an electric mixer on medium speed until thoroughly combined.

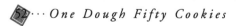

Divide the dough into 4 equal pieces and roll them out between sheets of wax paper to ⅛ to ¹⁄₁₆ inch thick. Leaving the doughs between the papers, stack them on a baking sheet and freeze for 10 minutes.

Working with 1 sheet of dough at a time, remove the top paper and cut the dough into 2-inch rounds, transferring them to a baking sheet. Repeat with the remaining sheets of dough. Gather and reroll the scraps, cutting out more cookies in the same manner.

Bake the cookies for 13 to 15 minutes, or until firm. Transfer the cookies to wire racks to cool.

# Cashew Cardamom Sandies

## MAKES ABOUT 5 DOZEN

*Sandies, or sand tarts, are crisp-tender cookies that get their "sandy"* texture and appearance from granulated sugar, also known as sanding sugar. Though classically made with pecans, the combination of cashews and cardamom give these sandies a delightful new twist.

*½ recipe Master Dough (page 1)*
*1½ cups chopped lightly salted roasted cashews*
*¾ cup sugar plus ¼ cup for sprinkling*
*¾ teaspoon ground cardamom*
*Lightly beaten egg whites*

Preheat the oven to 350°F.

In a large bowl, beat together the dough, cashews, ¾ cup sugar, and cardamom with an electric mixer on medium speed until thoroughly combined.

Roll the dough out between 2 sheets of wax paper to ¼ inch thick. Using a 2-inch-round cookie cutter, cut out the cookies and arrange them 1 inch apart on

Note: Cardamom is an aromatic spice used extensively in Indian cuisine in both sweet and savory dishes. The tiny seeds form within a white or green papery pod, and then are removed and crushed. Ground cardamom seeds are readily available in supermarkets. As with all spices, but particularly with this one, make sure your supply is fresh.

ungreased baking sheets. Brush the tops lightly with egg white and sprinkle with the additional sugar.

Bake the cookies for 20 to 25 minutes, or until golden. Transfer the cookies to wire racks to cool.

# Apricot Stars

$T$*hese cookies can be made in any shape you desire—rounds, flow-*ers, or diamonds. Fill them with your favorite jam or melted chocolate.

*½ recipe Master Dough (page 1)*
*⅔ cup apricot jam*

Preheat the oven to 350°F.

Divide the dough in half and reserve one half wrapped in wax paper or plastic wrap and chill. Roll out the remaining dough between 2 sheets of wax paper to ⅛ inch thick and freeze or chill on a baking sheet until firm, about 15 minutes.

Remove the top sheet of paper. Using a 1½- to 2-inch star-shaped cookie cutter, cut out stars, arranging them 1 inch apart on ungreased baking sheets. Gather and reroll the scraps, cutting out as many stars as possible.

Bake cookies about 10 to 12 minutes, or until pale golden. Carefully transfer the cookies to wire racks to cool. These will be the cookie bottoms.

Roll out, chill, and cut the reserved dough in the same manner as above. With a small star or round cutter, cut and lift out the centers of each star.

Note: Do not use unsweetened jams or fruit spreads, because the sugar content is needed for the centers to set and hold the cookies together.

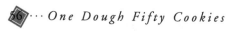

Bake the cookie tops in the same manner as above.

In a small saucepan, boil the jam, stirring, then simmer for 2 minutes, and strain through a fine-mesh sieve, pressing the solids through if possible. Arrange the whole stars, bottom sides up. Drop ¼ teaspoon of jam on each cookie, spreading it almost to the edges. Top each with a cutout star and spoon any remaining jam into the centers. Let the cookies stand until set. (The time it takes to set depends on the humidity and temperature of the kitchen. If it is very hot and humid, chill the cookies until set and store in an airtight container in the refrigerator.)

# Gingerbread Cutouts with Egg-Safe Royal Icing

## MAKES ABOUT 5 TO 10 DOZEN

*Finally, here is a gingerbread cookie that tastes as good as it looks.* There are cookie cutters in every shape imaginable on the market, so look for some unique ones—make an entire village for Christmas, spider webs for Halloween, Easter eggs, or maple leaves and pilgrims for Thanksgiving. Plus, they are the perfect place cards for table settings.

*½ recipe Master Dough (page 1)*
*1 tablespoon plus 1 teaspoon ground ginger*
*1 tablespoon plus 1 teaspoon ground cinnamon*
*¾ cup firmly packed brown sugar*
*½ teaspoon ground cloves*
*¼ teaspoon finely ground black pepper*
*1 recipe Egg-Safe Royal Icing (page 60)*

Preheat the oven to 350°F.

In a large bowl, beat together all the ingredients except the icing with an electric mixer on medium speed until thoroughly combined.

Note: If you don't have a pastry bag, you can spoon the icing into a sealable plastic bag, expelling the air, and with scissors snip off a tiny piece of the corner of the bag. Press the icing out the small hole, as you would with a pastry bag. The icing can be colored (and thinned) with food coloring and painted onto the cookies.

On a generously floured work surface, roll out the dough to slightly thinner than ¼ inch. Using the cookie cutter, cut out as many cookies as possible. Transfer the cookies with a metal spatula to an ungreased baking sheet. Gather the scraps and cut out more cookies.

Bake the cookies for 12 to 15 minutes, or until crisp. Transfer the cookies to wire racks to cool.

Fill a pastry bag, fitted with a fine writing tip, with the icing and decorate the cookies as desired.

# Egg-Safe Royal Icing

In recent years we have been aware of the dangers of salmonella bacteria present in raw eggs. Most food professionals have stopped using eggs where the final product is not fully cooked. Unfortunately, the versatile, nonfat egg white is not quite so versatile anymore.

In order to lighten mousses, tiramisù, or frozen soufflés, the whites must be heated to a certain temperature, which complicates these once-simple recipes.

Now there is a product widely available to the home cook, which was once only familiar to commercial bakers. Pasteurized dried egg whites are safe, convenient, and all natural. Look for it in a can in your local supermarket or health food store.

*¼ cup warm water*
*4 teaspoons pasteurized dried egg whites*
*3 to 3½ cups confectioners' sugar*

In a large bowl, whisk together the water and egg whites until dissolved. Beat the mixture until foamy and gradually beat in enough of the sugar to form an icing stiff enough to pipe onto cookies.

# Chocolate Hazelnut Pepper Rings and Holes

MAKES ABOUT 8 DOZEN

*Black pepper may seem like a strange ingredient for cookies, but* when paired with chocolate, it adds a deep, spicy, and rich flavor. Allspice is also a peppercorn, but one we are used to tasting in baked goods.

If all rings are desired, gather the scraps and reroll the dough.

*½ recipe Master Dough (page 1)*
*1 cup hazelnuts, chopped*
*⅓ cup unsweetened cocoa powder*
*⅓ cup firmly packed brown sugar*
*1 teaspoon finely ground black pepper*
*¾ teaspoon ground allspice*
*¾ teaspoon baking soda*

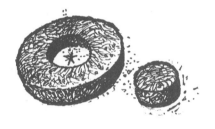

Preheat the oven to 350°F.

In a large bowl, beat together all the ingredients with an electric mixer on medium speed until thoroughly combined.

Roll out the dough between 2 sheets of wax paper to ¼ inch thick. With a doughnut cutter, cut out rings. (Or use a 1½- to 2-inch-round cutter and a ¾-inch-round cutter to cut out the middles.) Arrange the rings and holes ¾ inch apart on ungreased baking sheets. Gather the scraps and cut out more rings and holes.

Bake the cookies for 15 to 18 minutes, or until crisp. Transfer the cookies to wire racks to cool.

# Miniature Fresh Corn Scones

MAKES ABOUT 5 DOZEN

*These* versatile little biscuits are a welcome treat for breakfast, snacks, tea time, or dinner. They are similar to corn bread (the sweet variety) with the full-bodied taste of fresh corn and the crunch of cornmeal. Serve them warm or at room temperature, plain or with jam. They make a perfect addition to a buffet with eggs, ham, and fruit.

*1 cup fresh or thawed frozen corn kernels*
*½ recipe Master Dough (page 1)*
*1 tablespoon lightly beaten egg white*
*1 tablespoon baking powder*
*⅓ cup yellow cornmeal*
*Approximately 3 tablespoons sugar for sprinkling*

Preheat the oven to 400°F.

Purée the corn kernels in a blender or food processor, scraping down the sides frequently, until almost smooth.

In a large bowl, beat together the dough, egg white, baking powder, and cornmeal with an electric mixer on medium speed until thoroughly combined.

Scrape the dough onto a generously floured surface. (The dough will be very soft.) Sprinkle the dough generously with more flour, and with floured hands pat the dough out to ½ inch thick. Cut out rounds with a 1½-inch-round cutter dipped in flour. Transfer the rounds to ungreased baking sheets, arranging them ¾ inch apart. Gather the scraps and cut out more rounds.

Brush the scones lightly with water and sprinkle each with a generous pinch of sugar.

Bake the scones for 13 to 16 minutes, or until golden. Transfer the scones to wire racks to cool.

# Ginger-Spiced Date Daisies

## MAKES ABOUT 11 DOZEN

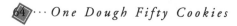

Turmeric is a vivid yellow spice often used as a cheap alternative to saffron in paella. It is used primarily in savory Indian dishes. Here, in addition to its lovely color, it adds a subtle exotic spiciness that complements the ginger.

½ recipe Master Dough (page 1)
1 cup chopped pitted dates
½ teaspoon ground turmeric
1¼ teaspoons ground ginger
¼ cup firmly packed brown sugar
¾ cup confectioners' sugar
1 tablespoon fresh lemon juice

Preheat the oven to 350°F.

In a large bowl, beat together the dough, dates, spices, and brown sugar with an electric mixer on medium speed until thoroughly combined.

On a floured work surface, roll the dough out in batches, each ¼ inch thick. Cut out flower shapes with a 2-inch cutter dipped in flour, arranging them ¾ inch apart on ungreased baking sheets.

Bake the cookies for 12 to 15 minutes, or until pale golden. Transfer the cookies to wire racks to cool.

In a small bowl, whisk together the confectioners' sugar and lemon juice until smooth. Drop a small dollop in the center of each cookie. Let the glaze set at room temperature before storing.

# Raspberry Hazelnut Diamonds

## MAKES ABOUT 8 DOZEN

*These cookies are rolled out and cut directly on the baking sheet.* They can be cut into whatever shapes are desired and there is no need to separate them before baking. It is the easiest cookie around!

*½ recipe Master Dough (page 1)*
*⅓ cup seedless raspberry jam*
*½ cup finely chopped hazelnuts or almonds*

Preheat the oven to 350°F.

On a large ungreased baking sheet, roll the dough out to ⅛ inch thick. Spread the dough with jam and sprinkle with nuts, patting them on very lightly.

Using a long, sharp knife or pizza cutter, cut through the dough, making parallel cuts about 1½ inches apart. Make more parallel cuts going across the first cuts at an angle to form diamonds.

Bake the sheet of dough for 15 to 17 minutes, or until it is pale golden. Let the sheet cool for 2 minutes. Recut the diamond shapes to separate them. Transfer the cookies to wire racks to cool completely.

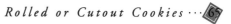

# DROP COOKIES

# Coconut Macaroon Butter Cookies

MAKES ABOUT 12 DOZEN

*B*ursting with coconut, these cookies differ from the classic maca-roon—they contain both butter and flour. This recipe can also be made using dry, unsweetened flaked coconut, which can be found in natural food stores or the natural foods section of your supermarket.

½ recipe Master Dough (page 1)
6 large egg whites
5 cups (about 14 ounces) sweetened flaked coconut
¾ cup sugar

Preheat the oven to 375°F. Grease the baking sheets.

In a large bowl, beat together all the ingredients with an electric mixer on high speed until thoroughly combined. Continue to beat until the mixture is light and fluffy.

Drop the batter by rounded teaspoonfuls 1 inch apart onto the pre-pared baking sheets.

Bake the cookies for 12 to 14 minutes, or until pale golden. Immedi-ately transfer the cookies to wire racks to cool.

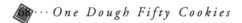

# Walnut Maple Syrup Cookies

These cookies are delightfully crisp and reminiscent of pralines. Either pancake syrup or pure maple syrup can be used, but pancake syrup actually gives a more pronounced maple taste, so save the good and expensive stuff for your pancakes!

½ recipe Master Dough (page 1)
⅔ cup pancake syrup or pure maple syrup
1½ cups walnuts, chopped
1 teaspoon baking soda

Preheat the oven to 350°F. Grease the baking sheets.

In a large bowl, beat together all the ingredients with an electric mixer on medium speed until thoroughly combined.

Drop the batter by rounded teaspoonfuls 2 inches apart onto the prepared baking sheets.

Bake the cookies for 14 to 17 minutes, or until golden. Let them cool on the sheets for 1 minute. Transfer the cookies to wire racks to cool.

# Chocolate Toffee Cookies

MAKES ABOUT 7 DOZEN

*T*hese cookies are a Southern praline and a brownie all in one—a marriage made in heaven!

*½ recipe Master Dough (page 1)*
*½ cup unsweetened cocoa powder*
*1 teaspoon baking powder*
*½ teaspoon baking soda*
*½ cup firmly packed brown sugar*
*3 large egg whites*
*1¾ cups (10 ounces) toffee or brickle bits*
*1 cup chopped pecans (optional)*

Preheat the oven to 350°F. Grease the baking sheets.

In a large bowl, beat together all the ingredients with an electric mixer on medium speed until thoroughly combined.

Drop the batter by rounded teaspoonfuls 2 inches apart onto the prepared baking sheets.

Bake the cookies for 12 to 14 minutes, or until the middles are set. Let the cookies cool on sheets for 1 minute. Transfer the cookies to wire racks to cool.

Note: Toffee bits are usually available in the baking section of markets, near the chocolate chips.

# Oatmeal Raisin Ginger Cookies

*These are the best of an oatmeal raisin cookie and a gingersnap rolled into one!*

*½ recipe Master Dough (page 1)*
*1½ cups old-fashioned rolled oats*
*½ cup molasses*
*½ cup firmly packed brown sugar*
*½ cup raisins*
*½ cup (3 ounces) crystallized ginger, chopped*
*1 teaspoon baking soda*

Preheat the oven to 350°F.

In a large bowl, beat together all the ingredients with an electric mixer on medium speed until thoroughly combined.

Drop the batter by rounded teaspoonfuls 2 inches apart onto ungreased baking sheets.

Bake the cookies for 14 to 17 minutes, or until golden. Transfer the cookies to wire racks to cool.

# Good, Old-fashioned Chocolate-Chip Cookies

## MAKES ABOUT 6 DOZEN

$A$*t my house you don't mess with chocolate-chip cookies. I wouldn't* dare add a nut or a raisin for fear of an uprising, although I personally have no objection. These are the thin, crisp, and chewy variety.

*½ recipe Master Dough (page 1)*
*1 cup firmly packed brown sugar*
*1 teaspoon baking soda*
*¾ teaspoon salt*
*¼ cup lightly beaten egg whites*
*2 cups chocolate chips*
*Nuts and raisins (optional)*

Preheat the oven to 350°F.

In a large bowl, beat together all the ingredients, except for the chocolate chips (and nuts and raisins, if using), with an electric mixer on medium speed until thoroughly combined. Stir in the chocolate chips and the nuts and raisins, if desired.

Drop the batter by rounded teaspoonfuls 2 inches apart onto ungreased baking sheets.

Bake the cookies for 12 minutes, or until pale golden. Transfer the cookies to wire racks to cool.

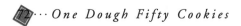

# Minted Lemonade Coolers

*R*efreshing and light, these delicate cookies get their zesty taste from lemonade concentrate. Here is a way to get intense lemon flavor without squeezing or grating.

*1 teaspoon dried mint leaves*
*½ cup frozen lemonade concentrate*
*½ recipe Master Dough (page 1)*
*¾ teaspoon baking soda*
*Approximately 1 cup confectioners' sugar*

Note: For extra tang, you can add ¼ teaspoon granulated citric acid to the confectioners' sugar. This is an ingredient often used in Middle Eastern cuisine and can be found in markets specializing in those ingredients as well as at some pharmacies. Citric acid is the ingredient that gives commercial lemon coolers and sour gummy candies their intense puckering quality.

Crumble the mint into a small bowl, add the lemonade concentrate, and mash the mixture together with a fork.

In a large bowl, beat together the dough, baking soda, and lemonade mixture with an electric mixer on medium speed until thoroughly combined. Wrap the dough completely in wax paper and chill for at least 8 hours or overnight.

Preheat the oven to 350°F. Grease the baking sheets.

Drop the dough by rounded ½ teaspoonfuls 1 inch apart onto the prepared baking sheets.

Bake the cookies for 13 to 17 minutes, or until pale golden. Transfer them to wire racks and sift confectioners' sugar generously on top. Let the cookies cool.

# Chocolate Trail Mix Clusters

## MAKES ABOUT 6 DOZEN

*Trail mix is a concoction of candy, nuts, and dried fruit. It was* invented to supply energy to those exerting themselves on a hiking trail, but you don't have to be breathing heavily to enjoy these chunky chocolate cookies! Any trail mix can be substituted for the chocolate-covered raisins or peanuts. M&M's, chocolate chips, or dried cherries or cranberries are just a few choices.

½ recipe Master Dough (page 1)
1 cup firmly packed brown sugar
1 teaspoon baking soda
¼ cup lightly beaten egg whites
⅓ cup unsweetened cocoa powder
1½ cups (10-ounce bag) chocolate-
    covered raisins
¾ cup unsalted or lightly salted peanuts
1 cup sweetened flaked coconut

Preheat the oven to 350°F.

In a large bowl, beat together the dough, sugar, baking soda, egg whites, and cocoa powder with an electric mixer on medium speed until thoroughly combined. Stir in the chocolate-covered raisins, peanuts, and coconut.

Drop the batter by rounded teaspoonfuls 2 inches apart onto ungreased baking sheets.

Bake the cookies for 12 to 15 minutes, or just until firm. Transfer the cookies to wire racks to cool.

# Pine Nut Almond Cookies

## MAKES ABOUT 8 DOZEN

*Pignoli are traditional Italian macaroon cookies. They are made* with almond paste and studded with pine nuts, but they contain neither flour nor butter. The flavors in this cookie were inspired by the classic one, but the texture is much more crisp and coarse.

½ recipe Master Dough (page 1)
3 large egg whites
¾ cup confectioners' sugar, plus additional for dusting the cookies
2½ cups blanched or natural almonds, finely ground
½ cup pine nuts
2 teaspoons almond extract
½ teaspoon baking soda
½ teaspoon salt

Preheat the oven to 350°F.

In a large bowl, beat together all of the ingredients with an electric mixer on medium speed until thoroughly combined.

Drop the batter by rounded teaspoonfuls 1 inch apart onto ungreased baking sheets.

Bake the cookies for 15 to 18 minutes, or until just firm to the touch (do not overbake). Transfer the cookies to wire racks to cool. Sift the additional confectioners' sugar over the cookies.

# Carrot Cake Cookies

## MAKES 7 DOZEN

$T$*hese spongy cookies will satisfy any carrot cake lover.*

¾ pound carrots, peeled
½ recipe Master Dough (page 1)
¾ cup firmly packed brown sugar
¾ cup chopped walnuts
¾ cup dried currants
1 teaspoon baking soda
1 teaspoon ground cinnamon

Preheat the oven to 350°F. Grease the baking sheets.

Cut the carrots into pieces and purée them in a food processor. Measure out 1½ cups of the purée, discarding any of the excess.

In a large bowl, beat together all of the ingredients, including the carrot purée, with an electric mixer on medium speed until thoroughly combined.

Drop the batter by rounded teaspoonfuls 1 inch apart onto the prepared baking sheets.

Bake the cookies for 13 to 16 minutes, or until springy to the touch (do not overbake). Transfer the cookies to wire racks to cool.

*Drop Cookies* ···

# BAR COOKIES AND BISCOTTI

# Tropical Blondies

□□□□ □□□□ □□□□ □□□□ □□□□ □□□□ □□□□
 • •   • • •   • • •   • • •   • • •   • • •   • • •

*C*hock-full of flavors from the tropics and garnished with a lime glaze swizzle, these white brownies are bound to shine!

*2 cups sweetened flaked coconut*
*One 8-ounce can crushed pineapple*
*½ recipe Master Dough (page 1)*
*1 cup granulated sugar*
*¼ cup lightly beaten egg whites*
*1 cup white chocolate chips*
*1 cup macadamia nuts*
*½ cup confectioners' sugar*
*1 tablespoon fresh lime juice*

Preheat the oven to 350°F. Grease and flour a 9 × 13-inch baking pan.

Spread the coconut in a large shallow baking sheet and bake, stirring occasionally, 5 to 8 minutes, or until partially toasted.

Drain the pineapple in a sieve and gently press out excess juice. In a large bowl, beat together the dough, granulated sugar, egg whites, coconut, and pineapple with an electric mixer on medium speed. Add the chocolate chips and nuts, and mix until thoroughly combined. Spread the batter in the prepared pan.

Note: Here is the trick to getting blondies (and brownies) out of the pan in perfect bars:

Always grease and flour the pan.

Always let them cool completely before cutting.

Bake for 35 to 40 minutes, or until pale golden and a toothpick inserted in the center comes out clean. Let the blondies cool completely.

In a small bowl, whisk together the confectioners' sugar and lime juice. Drizzle the glaze over the top of the blondies and let the glaze set.

Cut into 1- to 2-inch squares.

# Apricot Nut Biscotti

## MAKES ABOUT 6 DOZEN

Americans have not only caught on to Italian biscotti but they've also become addicted to these crisp, satisfying treats. In all fairness it should be noted that other cuisines, such as German and English, have long known the pleasures of these twice-baked cookies.

First the dough is formed into long logs and baked whole. Then the logs are sliced and baked again, producing uniform, crisp dry cookies, perfect for dunking in coffee or sweet wine. (Traditional Italian biscotti are often served with a dessert wine called Vin Santo.)

½ recipe Master Dough (page 1)
¼ cup lightly beaten egg whites
¾ cup cornmeal
½ cup honey
1½ cups dried apricots, chopped
1 teaspoon baking powder
1 teaspoon baking soda
1 cup chopped walnuts
¾ teaspoon grated orange zest

Preheat the oven to 350°F. Grease the baking sheets.
In a large bowl, beat together all the ingredients with an electric mixer on medium speed until thoroughly combined.

Divide the dough in thirds evenly and on the prepared baking sheet, form 3 logs with well-floured hands, each about 15 inches long.

Bake for 22 to 25 minutes, or until pale golden and firm to the touch. Let the logs cool on the sheet.

Transfer the logs to a cutting board and using a long serrated knife, cut them crosswise into ¾-inch-thick slices. Arrange the slices close together, but not touching, on ungreased baking sheets.

Bake for 12 to 15 minutes, or until pale golden and crisp. Transfer the biscotti to wire racks to cool.

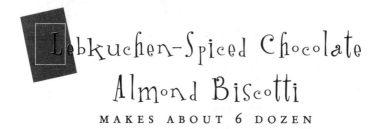

# Lebkuchen-Spiced Chocolate Almond Biscotti

### MAKES ABOUT 6 DOZEN

Lebkuchen is a traditional German cake or cookie made with a blend of spices used so often in baking that in Europe it is sold in pre-mixed packets as "Lebkuchen spices." Here they offer a new spicy twist to crisp biscotti. Bran is added to make a drier dough as well as to add texture and a little healthful fiber.

There is no need to turn the biscotti during the second baking, because they will dry and crisp as they cool.

½ recipe Master Dough (page 1)
¼ cup lightly beaten egg whites
½ cup unprocessed bran
½ cup firmly packed brown sugar
⅓ cup unsweetened cocoa powder
1¼ cups almonds, chopped
2 teaspoons baking powder
2 teaspoons aniseeds
2 teaspoons ground cinnamon
½ teaspoon ground ginger
⅛ teaspoon ground cloves
¼ teaspoon freshly grated nutmeg

Preheat the oven to 350°F. Grease a baking sheet.

In a large bowl, beat together all the ingredients with an electric mixer on medium speed until thoroughly combined.

Divide the dough in thirds evenly and on the prepared baking sheet, form 3 logs, each about 12 inches long.

Bake for 23 to 26 minutes, or until firm to the touch. Let the logs cool on the sheet.

Transfer the logs to a cutting board and using a long, serrated knife, cut them crosswise into ¾-inch-thick slices. Arrange the slices close together, but not touching, on ungreased baking sheets.

Bake for 15 to 20 minutes, or until toasted and crisp. Transfer the biscotti to wire racks to cool.

# Fudge Brownie Bars

## MAKES 4 DOZEN

A rich, fudgy layer of brownie sits atop a buttery cookie crust to make this treat a sinfully scrumptious indulgence. In order to get neatly sliced bars, let them cool completely before cutting. Remember, it is possible to have too much of a good thing, so cut them small.

*½ recipe Master Dough (page 1)*
*2 cups chocolate chips*
*⅓ cup firmly packed brown sugar*
*⅓ cup lightly beaten egg whites*

Preheat the oven to 350°F.

Measure 1 cup of dough into a dry measuring cup, packing it level with the rim, and press the dough onto the bottom of an ungreased 9 × 13-inch baking pan.

Bake the crust for 10 to 12 minutes, or until pale golden. Let it cool in the pan on a wire rack.

Set the bowl of an electric mixer over a saucepan of simmering water, add the chocolate chips, and stir until melted. Remove the bowl from the heat and add the remaining dough, sugar, and egg whites. Beat together with an electric mixer on medium speed until thoroughly combined. Spread the batter carefully over the crust.

Bake for 28 to 33 minutes, or until a toothpick inserted in the center comes out with no crumbs adhering to it. Let it cool completely.

Cut into 1½-inch squares.

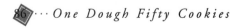

# Apricot Shortbread

□□□□□□□□□□□□□□□□□□□□□□□□□□□□□□□□

$D$ried apricots lend a tangy, chewy twist to this buttery, crisp shortbread. If you prefer, the shortbread can be baked in two 9-inch-round
cake pans, each lined with a round of parchment. Cut the shortbread
into small wedges for different shapes.

*½ recipe Master Dough (page 1)*
*¾ cup chopped dried apricots*
*¼ cup sugar*

Preheat the oven to 375°F. Line the bottom of a 9 × 13-inch baking
pan with parchment or wax paper.

In a large bowl, beat together the dough and apricots with an electric
mixer on medium speed until thoroughly combined.

Press the dough into the pan. Using a sharp knife, cut through the
dough, marking it into small squares or rectangles, and sprinkle with the
sugar. Prick the top all over with a fork.

Bake the shortbread for 30 minutes, or until golden brown around
the edges. Let the shortbread cool for 10 minutes. Invert the shortbread
onto a clean board, remove the paper, and recut the shortbread into bars.

# Crispy Rice Shortbread

**MAKES ABOUT 6 DOZEN**

$T$*he addition of crisp rice cereal to butter cookie dough produces a* rich shortbread with a satisfying crunch. A British friend of mine makes the best shortbread I've ever tasted. Her secret ingredient is rice flour, mailed to her twice a year from England. It adds a delicate dry crispness not attainable with plain wheat flour. The following shortbread packs a much larger crunch and, with the chocolate drizzle, tastes like a Nestle's Crunch bar.

*½ recipe Master Dough (page 1)*
*3½ cups crisp rice cereal*
*1 ounce semisweet, bittersweet, or milk chocolate,*
*    melted*

Preheat the oven to 350°F. Grease a 9 × 13-inch baking pan.

In a large bowl, beat together the dough and cereal with an electric mixer on medium speed until thoroughly combined.

Press the dough into the pan. Using a sharp, thin knife, cut through the dough, marking it into 1-inch squares.

Bake the shortbread for 25 to 30 minutes,

Note: For a simple way to melt and drizzle chocolate, put chocolate in a heavy sealable plastic bag. Leaving the bag open, heat in a microwave oven for about 30 seconds, or until just melted. Using scissors, snip off a corner of the bag to make a very small opening, and press the chocolate out the hole by twisting the bag. Drizzle it all over the surface of the shortbread.

or until golden brown around the edges. Let the shortbread cool for 10 minutes and recut the shortbread into squares. Drizzle with chocolate (see Note).

When the chocolate is set, carefully remove the squares from the pan and store in an airtight container with wax paper between the layers.

# Apple Graham Cracker Crumb Bars

## MAKES 4 DOZEN

□□□□ □□□□ □□□□ □□□□ □□□□ □□□□ □□□□
 • • •   • • •   • • •   • • •   • • •   • • •   • • •

H*ere the magnificent Master Dough is transformed into a crunchy* streusel topping as well as a buttery cookie crust. These apple crisp sweets are a great addition to the breakfast table or lunch box. They also make a nice dessert with a scoop of vanilla ice cream on the side. These bars freeze well, stacked in single layers between sheets of wax paper.

*2 Granny Smith apples*
*1 tablespoon fresh lemon juice*
*½ recipe Master Dough (page 1)*
*¾ cup graham cracker crumbs*
*¼ cup firmly packed brown sugar*
*1 teaspoon ground cinnamon*
*3 large egg whites*

Preheat the oven to 350°F. Grease and flour a 9 × 13-inch baking pan.

Peel, core, and chop the apples. In a bowl, toss them with the lemon juice.

Measure ¾ cup of the dough into a dry measuring cup, packing it level with the rim, and combine in a bowl with ½ cup of the graham cracker crumbs, the brown sugar, and cinnamon. Blend the mixture with fingertips until crumbly.

In a large bowl, beat together well the remaining dough, the remaining ¼ cup crumbs, and the egg whites with an electric mixer on medium speed. Spread the dough in the pan and top with the apples. Scatter the crumb mixture evenly on top.

Bake in the oven for 40 to 45 minutes, or until deep golden brown. Let the bars cool completely in the pan on a wire rack.

Cut into 1½-inch squares.

# Banana Raisinette Bars

### MAKES ABOUT 3 DOZEN

These cakelike bars make a tasty, energizing snack, delicious dessert, and even a breakfast treat. These are the best of chewy blondies and banana bread rolled into one. Chocolate-covered raisins are available in semisweet or milk chocolate, either of which will do.

*½ recipe Master Dough (page 1)*
*¾ cup mashed ripe bananas (about 2)*
*¾ cup firmly packed brown sugar*
*½ cup quick-cooking or old-fashioned rolled oats*
*1 teaspoon baking soda*
*1⅓ cups chocolate-covered raisins*
*1 cup chopped walnuts or peanuts (optional)*
*¼ cup granulated sugar*
*½ teaspoon freshly grated nutmeg*

Note: Overripe bananas can be peeled and frozen in freezer bags until ready to use. Just defrost and mash like fresh bananas. They are also perfect for milk or yogurt shakes.

Preheat the oven to 350°F. Grease and flour a 9 × 13-inch baking pan.

In a large bowl, beat together the dough, bananas, brown sugar, oats, and baking soda with an electric mixer on medium speed until thoroughly combined. Add the raisins and nuts, and beat until just combined. Spread the batter in the prepared pan and sprinkle with the granulated sugar and nutmeg.

Bake for 35 to 40 minutes, or until golden and a toothpick inserted in the center comes out clean. Let the bars cool completely on a rack.

Cut into 1- to 2-inch squares.

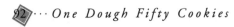

# Cookies for All Occasions

## CHILDREN'S FAVORITES/ COOKIE JAR CHAMPIONS

Classic Spritz Cookies
Jelly Bowls
Mocha Butter Balls
Malted Milk Buttons
Shattered Chocolate Balls
Granola Bars
Chocolate-Dipped Coconut Sticks
Graham Cracker Honey Washboards
Chocolate Marzipan Pinwheels
Peanut Butter and Jelly Sandwiches
Cinnamon Chocolate Moons
Deep Chocolate Wafers

Apricot Stars
Gingerbread Cutouts
Walnut Maple Syrup Cookies
Chocolate Toffee Cookies
Oatmeal Raisin Ginger Cookies
Good, Old-fashioned Chocolate-Chip
	Cookies
Chocolate Trail Mix Clusters
Carrot Cake Cookies
Fudge Brownie Bars
Crispy Rice Shortbread
Banana Raisinette Bars

## HAPPY HOLIDAYS

Classic Spritz Cookies
Jelly Bowls
Mocha Butter Balls
Orange Marmalade Walnut Pillows
Almond Crescents
Orange Date Oatmeal Crisps
Russian Tea Cakes
Rugelach Spirals
Apricot Stars

Gingerbread Cutouts
Raspberry Hazelnut Diamonds
Walnut Maple Syrup Cookies
Carrot Cake Cookies
Apricot Nut Biscotti
Lebkuchen-Spiced Chocolate Almond
	Biscotti
Apricot Shortbread

## EFFORTLESSLY ELEGANT AFTER-DINNER TREATS

Zesty Lime and Almond Sticks
Sambuca Coffees
Almond Crescents
Berry Gem Tartlets

Chocolate-Dipped Coconut Sticks
Cappuccino Wafers
Tangy Lemon Wedges
Bitter Chocolate Almond Cookies

Chocolate Marzipan Pinwheels
Rugelach Spirals
Cashew Cardamom Sandies
Chocolate Hazelnut Pepper Rings and
  Holes
Pine Nut Almond Cookies

Fudge Brownie Bars
Apricot Nut Biscotti
Lebkuchen-Spiced Chocolate Almond
  Biscotti
Apricot Shortbread

## PICNIC PLEASERS

Shattered Chocolate Balls
Granola Bars
Graham Cracker Honey Washboards
Bitter Chocolate Almond Cookies
Chocolate Marzipan Pinwheels
Malted Milk Buttons
Lemon Poppyseed Pillows
Deep Chocolate Wafers
Cashew Cardamom Sandies
Miniature Fresh Corn Scones
Coconut Macaroon Butter Cookies
Walnut Maple Syrup Cookies
Chocolate Toffee Cookies

Oatmeal Raisin Ginger Cookies
Good, Old-fashioned Chocolate-Chip
  Cookies
Chocolate Trail Mix Clusters
Carrot Cake Cookies
Tropical Blondies
Fudge Brownie Bars
Apricot Nut Biscotti
Apricot Shortbread
Crispy Rice Shortbread
Banana Raisinette Bars
Apple Graham Cracker Crumb Bars

## NEW FLAVORS AND TWISTS

Zesty Lime and Almond Sticks
Sambuca Coffees
Malted Milk Buttons
Spiced Peanut Currant Cookies
Cinnamon Chocolate Moons
Cashew Cardamom Sandies
Chocolate Hazelnut Pepper Rings
  and Holes

Miniature Fresh Corn Scones
Ginger-Spiced Date Daisies
Minted Lemonade Coolers
Tropical Blondies
Lebkuchen-Spiced Chocolate Almond
  Biscotti
Crispy Rice Shortbread

## SUMMER SWEETS

Zesty Lime and Almond Sticks
Lemon Poppyseed Pillows
Berry Gem Tartlets
Tangy Lemon Wedges
Benne Seed Honey Wafers

Cashew Cardamom Sandies
Raspberry Hazelnut Diamonds
Minted Lemonade Coolers
Deep Chocolate Wafers

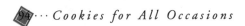

# Mail-Order Sources

*Sweet Celebrations/Maid of Scandinavia*
*P.O. Box 39426*
*Edina, MN 55439*
*(800) 328-6722*

*King Arthur Flour Bakers Catalog*
*P.O. Box 876*
*Norwich, VT 05055-0826*
*(800) 827-6836*

*Williams-Sonoma*
*P.O. Box 7456*
*San Francisco, CA 94120-7456*
*(800)541-2233*

# Index